STUPOR

STUPOR

poems

David Ray Vance

Elixir Press
Denver, Colorado

www.elixirpress.com

Book design by Steven Seighman
Cover art: "Frozen Charlotte" by Matthea Harvey

Library of Congress Cataloging-in-Publication Data

Vance, David Ray.
 [Poems. Selections]
 Stupor / David Ray Vance.
    pages ; cm.
 ISBN 1-932418-50-4 (alk. paper)
 I. Title.
 PS3622.A58594S78 2014
 811'.6—dc23
                              2013005053

        10   9   8   7   6   5   4   3   2   1

CONTENTS

STUPOR

For no apparent reason, a person may become mute, freeze for minutes or hours on end without any discernible awareness of the outside world, appear seemingly impervious to pain, and allow their limbs to be bent in all sorts of awkward positions... Is it simply due to something having gone terribly wrong in the person's brain, perhaps in areas responsible for movement? Or is the response one that has been bred into the human species for generations on end but was designed to deal with very different situations from the ones in which it is currently expressed?

Andrew K. Moskowitz
"'Scared Stiff': Catatonia as an Evolutionary-Based Fear Response."
(*Psychological Review*, 2004)

Prologue: At the Observation Pavilion

Ten days before admission you were not feeling well.

As if I were dead; I think I must have died.
The next morning you woke confused, frightened.

It seems I had been dead all the time.

When spoken to you smiled but would not open your eyes.
Sometimes I thought I was dead, other times I wasn't.

Your first week on the ward you said you were lost and damned.

I ought to have died but I fought it out.
You were seen smiling and again weeping.

I was sad and contented. I like it that way.

You were frightened and heard voices.
I died but I came back.

You thought there was a fire.

Give me water.
You thought there was shooting.

They knocked my head against the wall.

You said you wanted to die.
I died three times yesterday.

You became immobile and did not speak, eat or drink.

I don't think I could…
You reached a point where you did not care what happened.

I was dead all day.

Before the attack you sometimes said it got dark over your eyes.
Give me milk. Give me seltzer.

You said your face felt funny

I did not want to die myself.
You said the pain in your stomach had moved into your shoulder.

April fool—I kiss you seven kisses and one more.

You frothed at the mouth.
He is killing me.

For years you lay with your head covered, mute, tube-fed.

Holy father, white horse uncle.

This Poem Will Steal Your Breath As You Dream Red Tigers

Stretched out on a green savannah south of the equator
canopies of white linen overhead and a man fanning you
with palm leaves, a man you call *my dear, dearest love*
whose eyes never leave you once, even as the big cats
bound the distance between you and them, between now
and the moment they pounce with claws and incisors
ravenous for flesh, your lover turned spectator smiling
for he too would devour you given opportunity
his hands still waving the green palm fronds as red
speckles the savannah, his face vicious with love or desire
or whatever you call these peculiar, carnal appetites
carried into your dreams by you who would consume
and be consumed, you who have no lover whatsoever
who have never seen a tiger, caged or wild except
in dreams and then always of the brightest, reddest hue.

Character

Neuroses can be traced back to conflict
how fathers story voices finely wrought

      a cogent common-sense sketch of complex
      classical techniques in search of an author

educating hearts and minds; this is true
freedom, when we see every eulogium

      instantly recognizable the province
      of thinking persons: saints & scoundrels

other contradictory, inscrutable, enigmatic
real people empirically human, yet in fiction

      emotion & viewpoint trouble day by day
      both their racism and their denial

seven secrets, nine essential algebras
knowledge of modules and representations

      ordinary traits and exercises crafting
      dynamic tests for modern relationships

ready-to-use intimacy compelling precisely
because moral education seeds design

      multiplying influence, defining technique
      beyond handbook and classification

no attempt made to identify a finite
number of theoretic commandments

       politics makes and breaks prosperity
       family ills such as crime, poverty, pollution

terrorism and corruption sowing
a legacy for the helping professions

       constricted connection, compassion
       richly enduring spiritual significance

dramatic forerunner of life-shaping vision
this wondrous satisfied universe

       some reflection included.

Watchful We

Wind wistfully our way through this city without hands.
Honk horns with our hapless foreheads.
Force Funkadelic LPs into tape decks with feet and teeth.
Talk trash to our passengers, Israeli then Palestinian.
Pay parking tickets in pennies, dimes and nickels.
Negotiate nearly every hostage's return at the rendezvous.
Read Rousseau backwards, Kafka front to back.
Break bottles in alleyways beneath a phaseless moon.
Mold metal bumpers in maple-paneled garages.
Give gravity a run for its guilder, a currency not on offer.
Order ordinal numbers into a series of detonations.
Drink Dramamine shots—doubles—on ice.
Idle indignantly at stoplights flashing ganglion signs.
Sing soulfully, loud as we can, louder even.
Enter early twilight entirely unrepentant.
Unite under colored flags, until our motors up and quit.
Quiet quadriphonics not quite by choice.
Commit carpool offenses punishable by cash fine or jail.
Justify juvenile misconduct, adjudicate its violence.
Verify vicariously our long-lived limitations.
Litigate licensing procedures like full-fledged attorneys.
Award alternate status to all parking zealots.
Zoom-zoom the zero-down adverts of our youth.
Yield yearly revenues by multiplying y and x.
X-ray xerox copies at x-rated kiosks.
Kiss karma goodbye knowing nothing of wonder.

Patient I: So The Day Begins

The notice indicates a building and room, neither of which exist.

*Ms. Ergo wanders hours before taking a seat in some institutional
structure seemingly chosen at random (herself and the building).*

*Asked to complete a family history and to chronicle any preexisting
conditions she assumes a stranger's identity but becomes distraught
when unable to conjure her mother's face.*

*Note the candle wax on her shoe, a spot near the right toe.
These are new shoes and she has not been near a candle
or in the vicinity of one that she knows…*

*Every action appears momentous. And the one after that.
And the one after that.*

Absolutes Almost Always Run Afoul of Beauty

but barely anybody bothers to calculate
cost contingencies lest cash deficits

      drastically degrade consumer exuberance
      excluding entails formulated by elite fiscal

fact-finding missions we forgo all grants
guaranteed gratis by grandiose hierarchies

      heretofore heralded despite hourly ignominies
      intentionally ignoring intelligence jobbers

juking jail and job stats that jeopardize our kin
kept kowtowed by knickerbocker lawyers

      lackadaisically lyrical, their maledicted
      morals more or less money-driven, not novel

nor nearly so, but also not obfuscated
or obviously quick to order perpetrated

      petty practical jokes as private querulous
      quomodocunquizers quite capably remind

remonstrators reworking retrospective signs
since severe greed forms tongue twists

      tantamount to a trial, our universe
      uninterested unless ubiquitous variegated

viewpoints versify sin as when vile whale
watchers wrestle their white leviathans, x–rayed

      xenophobics xeric where xerophytes yellow
      yet you can't trade your yen for zygotes

zealously zapped by zymotic axioms

What I Say What?

Gone   crazy native fishing wild west mad
with the wind
swept turbine energy
crunch efficient

led   by the nose astray down the garden
path to water
drenched wheel works
miracles wonders
why

axis   powers of evil
intentions incarnate genius eye
blink candy spy lashes
forty

two   in the hand toned timer times the pleasure
dome palace principle
figure

drawing on our resources paper tablet water stares
cross-hatch
a plan a bird
dropping nest flu
in the hand

held   hostage in the bosom of the lord aloft
accountable in the highest esteem
building boiler jack
hammer 'o'lantern

lit   fuse from within torch
                light bearers songs
                      a penny each sung
                            live a capella
                            from the heart

felt   for others clammy claustrophobic
                weary sick
                    room in the head of you
                          bend turn my only
                                one.

§

This Poem Lies

Like anyone who ever promises to *always, forever, never*
whatever they swear, at least if we take them on their word
if time is a constant not relative the speaker's experience
so that *always, forever* and *never* need mean more than *so long*
as I live and don't lose my faculties, my perceived autonomy,
my will to live, my memory of you and what I've said, so long
as I persist without alteration which is impossible, change being
inevitable so that all oaths are doomed, I swear it's true
on this poem's grave and on the grave of every poem
which begat this poem, so on and etc., world/word
with or without end, so long as poems live and breathe
and we, weeping, clasp their reed-thin, deathly hands
with or without end, so long as poems live and breathe
which begat this poem, so on and etc., world/word
on this poem's grave and on the grave of every poem
inevitable so that all oaths are doomed, I swear it's true
as I persist without alteration which is impossible, change being
my will to live, my memory of you and what I've said, so long
as I live and don't lose my faculties, my perceived autonomy
so that *always, forever* and *never* need mean more than *so long*
if time is a constant not relative the speaker's experience
whatever they swear, at least if we take them on their word
like anyone who ever promises to *always, forever, never*

Modern Life

Ordinary people far from undermining life
                    after death in ancient Istanbul
changed the rhythm and often place of myth

            a refuge against unempirically precious
lives commodified in synch with market
                    imperatives lost in Paris entirely

the range of practical problems untroubled
            by genuine physical or psychological ironies
made great simple-hearted idealists

                    the best captured in what
psychiatrists call life events, our experiments
            creating space articulate difficulties

of both identity and identification
                    contemporary aesthetic rejected
village life traditions leaving

        the reader ravaged and anguished
unable to express achieved greatness
                    man himself as one critic put it

the most magnificent and original
            invention become almost machine
information meets sensibilities associated

        with culture's many expectations
in practice to forestall death as materialism
      our species reduced beneficially

equates geological archea
        with microbial processes secondary
knowledge of scientific experience.

The Somnambulist Awakens To Discover

Both cars parked on front lawn
        keys in their ignitions, radios tuned
            to the same AM station

twelve e-mails accepting an e-vite
        for *"high tea at high noon
            b-y-o-herrings, bitches"*

refrigerator door off its hinges
        cat asleep in the crisper drawer
            cat litter in the butter tray

half-baked soufflé in the oven
        topped with diced dill pickle
            and ipod earbuds

right ear newly pierced
        left eyebrow clean shaven
            favorite shoes in toilet

dining room window wedged open
        with a coffee table leg, tabletop
            nailed to ceiling

TV remote missing and a ransom note
        written in pseudo-Portuguese
            glued to the screen

circular bruises on both forearms
        what look like infinity symbols
            size of duck eggs.

Some Nights I Expire

Into a quadrillion teensy threads of light each less brilliant than the preceding day's endoscopic journey through graying matter materially indifferent to the coconut-sized anxieties weighting down my dream life textured like spackle or double clotted cream but in either case far less tasty and less pleasing to the touched angels veiled in sleep deep beneath colossal bridge abutments south of this mammoth regret we call a city where those same wingless verities daily push invisible carts packed skyward past car-parks pleading invidiously for relief in whatever form or incarnation it presents whether disease or symptom diagnostics a naming ceremony awry with accusations of malingering malevolent malfeasance however the callous beating nestled in our sternums the drum that responds and calls percussive as footfalls on the continental landing.

Natural Light

Your body forms full where you remember
shadows' edges no longer

      evocative the pineal gland in the brain
         glowing suffused darkness

bones' hollow panoramic views

            [deeper structures
            interior and exterior
            conceal word images
            anti-parasitic, anti-
            inflammatory]

  natural law an assemblage of fabrics that filter
and tint the rest of the century

              formed by doctrine
        the existing black hole prism
           polarized to modify or enhance
           a 100-watt filament

hence extremely light with mauvish patches

       heathland and sand rises
          out of the watery blueness
     too narrow to fill the pupil

predictable timing of leaf color, dark to light
observed within dreams

> [a spherical flask
> burning amid
> prolonged chlorophyll
> saturation]

this first dusk upon us, tiny red world.

Elementals

Made air, made water, made the fire worry scheming hands.
Made the stench drift over the wall from the neighbor's dim plot.
Made the white lye burn the whites of our collective eyes.

And the man who climbs the wall. And the child in his arms.
And the tortures the child will endure at the hands of this man.
Made rock, made soil, made the sand we grit between teeth.

The castles that crown our teeth. The eyes our teeth see with.
The teeth we chew. Grounded wires riddled with current
to grind every nerve. Sockets blossoming red hemorrhage.
Our temples and brows crowned in scepters of blood.

And the man who climbs the wall. And the child in his arms
two hands clenched into fists. Skin ravaged where knuckles
scraped brick. And the tortures the child will endure at the hands
of this man or some other man. The puncture an incisor makes.

The rupture that is a child's scream. Made rock, made soil,
made sand. Made the white lye dusted over us. And the teeth
we see with. The teeth we chew. Made air, made water...

This Poem Will Save Our Lives

Blindfolded, shackled in a windowless concrete room
when the interrogator pauses to light another cigarette

to wipe the sweat-smear from his horn-rimmed glasses
and dials up the electrodes clipped to our nipples

his back a cobra's hood overshadowing our naked forms
we will remember this pathetic little excuse of a poem

will recite it verbatim in our minds, every line crisp
despite the deafening temple-throb, despite the sickly

shudder that ripples from our cheeks down our necks
through shoulder and erector muscles, lodging itself

in the hollow of our shattered left patellas; we will
remember this mean blood clot of verse and pray

that its prophecy fails us. *Please*, we'll whimper, *please…*

Victory and Opposites

He made no attack the lucky man
braced to meet a darkness spreading

      visibly behind the opposite dyke
      inside he felt a cold black explosion

sackful of debt marching a cordon
from Toungoo to Nyaunglebin

      opposite of a nova dreamed
      how fragile chronological experience

transcendence wrought where bridges
were blown and a suitcase

      space on the opposite side pierced air
      with principles paradoxical

hours later beaten by Japanese guards
below decks in your mind

      the previous time period opposite
      remnants in his vest pockets

ceremonial bronze ax proclaiming
two innocuous sentences

      between opposite members of the sex
      communication dialectical

expressions of allegiance metaphor
framed actuality.

By Definition

Bruises are blood beneath the skin, in time drained or absorbed
by living tissue. Postmortem they linger until flesh decays
become loci for decomposition.

                On the High Streets people transform
consumers of goods/good consumers, shadowless reflections
on shop windows.

          "purchase" a simile for hold
          "product" a quantity obtained by multiplication

Streets become roads, turn superhighways, metaphors
for information systems more or less systematic than we dare admit
even in the privacy of our shuttered minds.

Hence, you anticipate a reference, philosophical or what have you
law of the land being word made flesh, blue-black beneath its surface.

Goods are valueless, values expressions. We do not hold them so much
as factor in their possibility.

      When I tell you secrets they cease being secrets.

              Like facts they are tenuous, temporal,
the known lost within the limits of knowledge, diminished
by its status as such; but raw material from which we manufacture
principles, abutments built upon the superstructure, wrought beneath
its incalculable mass.

Never underestimate the influence of operant conditioning.
Even now the body resists its casket.

Extra-Extra (Ordinary Rendition):

Confidential informant reported that subject frequents an establishment associated with known discordant elements

Pursuant to instructions, agents followed subject at some distance, entered said business and positioned themselves inconspicuously near both exits

Agents noted that subject took no notice of their presence

Subject proceeded to order a red liquid refreshment of unknown origin ornamented with pink umbrella; its significance, uncertain at the time, remains unascertained

Of principal import was fact that subject wore gray and black including a beret (see enclosed photographs)

Given the tense political climate, and in light of subject's provocative attire, agents determined supplementary scrutiny warranted

At a local eatery later that same evening, subject read a volume of poetry while eating a distinctly middle-eastern vegetarian sandwich

Subject was immediately apprehended and air-ferried to foreign jurisdiction X-23 for coercive interrogation

Despite risk of public protest (public safety being paramount), the bureau "advocates indefinite clandestine incarceration without trial or tribunal" as is reasonable and justified

We Are At War

with prepositions, all
relative position

forever undoing the yet
unrealized

to "anticipate" change

that might not ever
the photograph
underdevelops, disappoints

other thwarted potentials
we rejoice recognizing

existence outside immediate
lived experience

how things get done
and so described

categorical histories
transmitted atonally

to "speak plainly"
is to say a previous
understood.

Night Terrors: Men Watch (and Women)

A man hacks another man's forehead with a cleaver. Blood is seen
on his face, also brains. A man gets his arms sawn off.
Lots of blood sprays on the wall. A man literally blows people up.
Blood, guts, and bone fragments are on the ceiling.
A man attempts to rape a woman, and he beats her in the process.
He is interrupted and punched a few times, his nose broken.
A man is brutally beaten then thrown out a window.
His twisted leg lies in a pool of blood. A man shoots a woman
in the thigh, then shoots off her fingers. John Kennedy's
assassination is seen from a distance so that it's hard
to tell what is going on but it is clear what happened. Some thugs
follow a man and woman into an alley. There is a fight.
We see two compound fractures: an elbow pops out in slow motion
and a man's leg is broken in half. Also some bloody faces.
A man shoots a pregnant woman, killing her. A man gets hot oil
poured on his face. A city is destroyed by a weapon
of mass destruction, but we see nothing particularly gory.
A man gets impaled by a grappling hook. In two scenes, men are lit
on fire. Dogs are shown fighting over a dead girl's leg.
People are tortured, their fingers broken or dislocated. The fingers
aren't seen but you hear them crack and hear screaming.
A man is shown dying of cancer. Two young men make crude
sexual remarks about a boy's mother. The boy strikes
one young man with a hammer, and tackles the other, biting his face.
We see the boy's bloody mouth, skin in his teeth.

Pi: A Drama With Theatrical Limits

3.1415 [...]
026535
097932

084626 Numbers fandango the stage on stilts of fire juggling burning orbs.
033832 They cha-cha and shimmy. They tell jokes at one another's expense.
095028
041971

093993
051058 During intermissions they gossip taking turns to whisper in my ear
009749 the offenses of this *one* or that *two* or those *six hundred thousands*.
045923

078164
062862 Many are overburdened with guilt and prone to confession.
089986
080348

053421 *I counted the intended victims* says one figure.
070679 *I counted their bodies after the fact* echoes its doppelganger.
021480

065132
023066 They are a patchwork a mosaic and I recognize in them patterns
070938 of color and light.
46095

05822
17253 The figures they transect are themselves transected and layered.
94081 They are a multitude of groupings.
84811

74502
41027
19385 Some have distinct odors. Others I taste on my tongue.
11055
96446

29489 When they speak I salivate. When they lie my right eye
49303 waters and twitches.
19644

88109
56659

[...]

Each day is divided is multiplied is square-rooted. Each exactly like those that preceded it yet nevertheless distinct.

From my place in the orchestra pit I stare up at them the angle dizzying so that we swing together from the rafters.

A machine backstage runs the calculations. It serves me but I am no one's master. I influence but do not control.

The cords that bind us are knotted and fused. They upbraid us. But by dent of certain operations we sometimes loose ourselves from their tangle.

Figures are hoisted into the rigging to be lowered on cue. Do not call them puppets. They pull my strings as I pull theirs. We bow and bend to one another. Curtsey and parry.

Not that liberation is possible. We cannot escape the theater.

There are no exits. There is nowhere to go.

[...]

Repetition is a matter of recognition and opinion.

My own opinion is it doesn't matter whether the show goes on
or where it goes or whether it arrives.

I keep my opinions to myself mostly. They hardly matter.

Same goes for the actors on the stage. They are numbers
and innumerable. They are individuals and a cast.

They reel out their soliloquies en masse.
They flounder in the net of my perception.

In theory they comprise a single spectacle.

Only occasionally I realize I've been speaking aloud
that some utterance has escaped me unintentionally.

I mean that literally. Escaped without my notice or know-how.
How these speech acts impact my condition who can say?

Only that singularly spectacular what-have-you can't help
but be parsed into acts for convenience sake.

465495
353710
507922
796892

It's convenient for all involved to parse them.
To act in that singular way.

589235
420199
561121
290219

508640

That we which is I. This I who tells you "I am the *all involved*"
that my *I* is plural. As if there were an option.

344181
598136
97747
13099

Division is inevitable and we inevitably conceive of parts
as distinct. Linked but separated.

505187
72113
99999

We praise them as such. Pray for them.

83729
80499
10597

Whether a form of transubstantiation or an exercise in variable
substitution such mental calculus requires denial of relation.
A local anesthetic.

17328
60963
85950

It's less aesthetic than acetic. Maybe I mean acidic?
Or acerbic?

44594
53469
83026
25223

[...]

82533
46850
52619

The wings are perpetually filled to capacity with performers
waiting their turns. They are desperate for attention most of them.
Hungry for a moment's recognition.

11881
10100
31378
87528
65875

They do not speak to one another but concentrate on their routines
mumbling over lines of dialogue or reciting tongue twisters
to limber up visualizing their marks on the stage.

32083
14206
71776
91473

35

035982 Those with more physical acts stretch themselves out
534904 some to the point that they are no longer numbers
287554 but some sort of ancient hieroglyphic.
687311
595628
638823 During scenery changes I pad about the pit or venture up
537875 to the balcony for another perspective.
937519
577818
577805
321712 From this vantage the scene is framed by curtains and the chaos
268066 backstage no longer visible.
130019
278766
111959 One can concentrate on the performances rather than their
092164 workings. One can surrender to the illusion.
201989
380952
572010 But to say there are no exits is to deny the stage its wings.
654858 Without them the show would never fly.
632788
559361
533818
279682 Without us it would burst into flame and suffocate
303019 on its own ash.
520353
018529
589957 The audience collectively singing out FIRE in unison.
736225 Like any other execution. A bullet to the heart.
394138 Another centered in the blindfold.
012497
217752
334791 Look it up in your program. It's right there.
315155 Pinned to my chest.
748572
424541
506959
508295

[...]

Not infrequently I weary of these spectacles these melodramas.
I am committed to my role as director as pit-boss whatever
my title. Yet I am susceptible to malaise.

To regain perspective I lock my eyes on an a dim patch of scenery.
A painted window or interior wall. Props or pieces
of stage furniture.

The figures dissolve into the periphery. They are present but no
longer dominate my perception.

Their show goes on though I am myself only vaguely aware.

This feat requires all my concentration and I can accomplish it
only seconds at a time.

I do not count the seconds. That would defeat the purpose.

§

This Poem Will Put Hair On Your Chi-Chi

Read at your own extreme risk.

Side Effects of this Poem May Include: *angina, blood pressure changes, burning or irritation of the eye, changes in cardiac output, in left ventricular mass, in pulse rate, chest pain, dermatitis, diarrhea, dizziness, eczema, edema, exacerbation of hair loss / alopecia, facial swelling, fainting, fast heartbeat, generalized hypertrichosis, headache, increases in left ventricular end-diastolic volume, irritant dermatitis, itching, light-headedness, nausea, palpitations, pericardial effusion, pericarditis, redness or irritation at the treated area, rhinitis, salt and water retention, severe allergic reactions (difficulty breathing, hives, itching, rash, swelling of the mouth, face, lips, or tongue, tightness in the chest,), sudden, unexplained weight gain, swollen hands or feet, tachycardia, tamponade, unwanted hair growth elsewhere on the body, visual disturbances including decreased visual acuity, vomiting.*

Field Stone

Chakras sheltered several children
exciting cemetery symbolism and iconography

  after lunch each day while the notion
  of eclectic experimentation rested

added art to cists known as kistvaens
box-like like stone coffins

  written and photographed along old fencerows
  come to know grass and wild flowers

against well-built layers some of which swirled
near ponds to accent a tall vertical

  sign by a gate of wood intruding
  tundra would starve a vagrant if he wasn't

back in time raving at me for trying
the character and inner purity hardest to build

  bottom to top laying down patterns
  I had no thought to see what surprises religion

lava cools down becomes volcanic rock
with permanent magnetic imprint

  scattered about towns opening up psychic
  order to the gardens along one end

chosen for what amounts to a suicide mission
visible people taking short cuts

     in the sea cliffs created when farmer Laronde
     attempted to plow the subconscious

sometimes breaking down a rare attribute found
at the base of a freshly dug foundation

     built in the early bronze of Bab edh-Dhra
     geology above-ground dark blue

song's puzzling parts your dog helped land
a deal of northwestern existence.

Fate of Humanity

The thought of appearing foolish
still scares us, a position of rational moderation.

Or if excess is our fate, demon of mine
have you suffered a hard fate at the housefly planet?

Seventy-five human beings become Gods
thieve and plot and toil and plod
our cosmic future, our destiny.

Those government leaders who pilot the ship
on a visit to humanity's ancient home
present in their historical times
an international organization destined
5 billion years to shape that blind
wrath of God which must meet natural selection
same as animals.

Success or failure bears only those
who control over anyone when the immediate
but related ideas of cosmopolitan observers
challenge the committee's stranglehold
and our ability to transform.

We must find a way to live with bottom-line
conflict-inducing adamantine chains
and ferocious hopelessness become anxieties
about the future, its tribulations
emblematic of transcendent forces.

Defining pastimes blind people of different images
and cultures—the contemporary freakish
paradox—phased out though without divinity
simply the ultimate fantasy
of a deluded species in crisis.

The metaphor of contagion illustrates more clearly
an embodied form inherent in our cultural life
a mere biological speck, especially in remoter ages
informed and motivated by disinterested relics
whose entire universe in general had been drawn
through an awakening awareness.

At The Time Of Perfect Description

When litotes swarmed intercontinental
        their eyes skyward gazing at smoke
                mink stoles or stolen goods sold

and rentals were not so steepled
        that filled miniscule bird lungs
                on bad market days hazed in clouds

we couldn't parse words days on end-
        with phosphour, dire days they were
                chiastic like feta-brine, seasonal

stopped-rooftop rhyme remembering
        our laughter crowded into boxcars
                nostalgia grinding personal axes

those wistful publican houses
        at rural junctures the tinctures
                and machetes to scalpel sharpness

their signs, bunting-wrapped, crudely-
        of anacoluthon redrawn
                unfettered by irrepressible survival

painted farm animals more human than
　　　　boundary stone, synonymia a mania
　　　　　　　　instincts, slipknot ellipses, tipsy

our men with their biceps bound
　　　　unapologetically parrhesian
　　　　　　　　authority, tongue tied, fork-tipped

in blue-black crepe, the train station
　　　　like these Parisan summers
　　　　　　　　double basses swaying arrhythmic

congregation plagued by steam
　　　　paradisiacal if paradiastole
　　　　　　　　beats down to ashes

Patient 2: Beating the Devil's Tattoo

*Age thirty-three, Mr. Sum is shot in his right foot, the round fired
by a neighbor intent on suicide.*

*Glancing shots are not uncommon; even modest public libraries
hold multiple volumes cataloging their several varieties
replete with vector diagrams illustrating trajectories
by which a bullet might crease a skull rather than smash it
or how a rib might deflect and not shatter or give way.*

*One imagines their authors escaped death in some like manner
—or had lovers who did not—and so arrived at this
singular obsession, but Mr. Sum's neighbor will never author
such a text.*

*He did his research, and so angled the barrel between his teeth
so that the bullet entered his soft pallet and pierced directly
offending brain matter, his skull exploding a thousand
splintery shards.*

*Momentum bore the bullet through sheetrock ceiling and wood
floorboard, lodging it finally in Mr. Sum's shallow, right arch.*

*The wound requires only six stitches but Mr. Sum forever after
recounts the story at dinner parties, and in later years
affects a severe limp.*

*On his deathbed he confesses to his only daughter that this one
experience—more than any other—gave his life meaning.*

A Problem of Localization: Leaving vs. Relocating

You pack bags, not boxes, and your mail is forwarded. Keep your library card, your local gym membership, the dentist's reminder. Worry the kettle on the stove, the light in the bathroom, the key still in the back door. Night before your departure, you imagine flames licking your private letters, your stash of mildly pornographic postcards, the not-so-gold fish in their perpetually murky bowl. Next day, you park in the long-term lot, the long and short of it relative the cab fare you might otherwise have spent. In the airport lounge you scrupulously mind your own business. Even as you hand over your ticket, you plan-hope-desire-expect to see again all you leave behind. Including the regret which follows you down the swaying gangway and onto the airplane, only to jettison itself midway through the in-flight flick. Don't fret. It will be waiting at the terminal upon your return. Wearing bunny ears, strap-on goggles and a leather aviator's cap. Dragging behind itself parachutes of blood.

§

This Poem Will Never Be Reprinted

No one will memorize this poem or transcribe it into their copybook. No one will place a laminated photocopy in their shower to contemplate between rinses. Most readers will not read it in its entirety. The phone will ring or the pot on the stove will boil. Or some other regret will well up inside them as they recall any number of things they've been meaning to read or attend to, things far more substantial. And those who do will forget it immediately. What is there to remember? No theorem for spiritual enlightenment. No reaffirmations on death or love or the death of love. This poem is a stranger passed in some foreign city, the one who points you to the nearest newsstand or bus stop. The same person you couldn't pick out of a line-up an hour later if your life depended on it, which it always does. But that's another story. One that has no place in this poem. And now, so many lines [lives? lies?] in, you waver, uncertain whether to continue. Who can blame you? Not the poem. It never asked to be written. As for me, I washed my hands of it before you arrived on the scene. I've obliterated my fingerprints with acid, had my face surgically altered. Besides, you don't know me from Adam. Besides, its too late. The end-time approaches. Hurry up, please. Fast. Now. Stop.

Shut Down Up

Seven years later the economic recession
opening hasty back door compromises

        potential production reluctantly scratched
        another mission the same size side-to-side

dozens of factories and businesses tried
acupuncture, cortisone injections potent

        force for continued change thin excuse
        when it comes time the tape readily erased

using Kitchener stitch to graft the opening
if that does not work look avenged

        supply electricity to the whole observatory
        of dustiest annals a short self-help manual

these bits of lost memory confusing cause
and the signed person angling little dramas

        for three hopes climbed out the cockpit
        physical body and emotions overloaded

in an attempt to overcome slow skilled
poorly volunteers, charitable and gentle

        signifies we must own our past generous
        steel mill seizures depression befallen

the city since its interface confusion
before the vision-occluding strobes

     a small ripple of satisfaction discovered
     hot little hand shrugged into his jacket

instructed us to walk single file before
oil spilled over the holding tanks again

         again summon this picture conflict
         eliminate it from our lives or control

I don't care what new culture you're in
lean on what we experience speaking

     words when we picked them dead.

Night Terrors: Dahlia Juarezii

We see a female body on a morgue table. We see her body is cut in half at the waist, her face cut ear to ear. There is a puncture wound on the palm of her hand, and we are told that her reproductive organs were removed but no rape occurred. It appears her nipples were cut off. Her knees were broken, and her body, drained of blood, was washed. We see the same dead body at a crime scene and hear about disembowelment, facial lacerations. A crow lands on the body and prepares to peck. A woman is hit hard twice with a baseball bat. Her head is clamped into a vice, and her face is sliced with a knife. We see the blade cutting and blood pours from the wound. A man attacks another man from behind with piano wire. Another man approaches and slashes the victim's throat with a knife. Blood sprays, and we see this scene again. Both the injured man and the man holding the wire fall off a balcony and crash into a fountain below. One man's head hits a fountain and splits open. Blood sprays and fills the fountain. We see crime scene photos of a woman with deep cuts from the side of her mouth to her ear. A woman shoots herself in the head. Blood sprays on the curtains behind her. A woman is shot, she falls back, and blood pools under her. A man is shot in the head and lies dead with blood pooling around him. We see a dead child with a bullet hole in his head and a dead man with blood on his face and neck. A woman finds a dead body on the side of a street. We see a nude form from a great distance. We see two dead bodies put into an incinerator. We see a blood-soaked mattress and a clump of hair in a vice. We see the initials of a man carved into a woman's back. Two men box, and one man is punched repeatedly while pinned in the corner. One man is cut over the eye. One man has his two front teeth knocked out. A police officer chases a man, tackles, and punches him. A man punches another man and threatens him with a gun. A man is hit on the back of the head with a gun. In a street shootout a man standing outside a building is shot and two police officers start shooting at people inside the building. Later we see dead bodies with bloody wounds. A man shoots a gun out a window and kills a pigeon. People fight in the streets. Several use heavy sticks as weapons. We see cars in flames, and hear of problems between "Zootsuiters" and service men. We are told that a man shot his family dog to consecrate the moment when he became a millionaire. We hear that a man's sister was murdered and the crime never solved. We hear police describing crimes including rape and other violent acts. We hear that a woman was badly beaten by a man. An earthquake shakes a building, and people hold on to items on desks and shelves until the tremor passes. A woman is frightened by a scene in a movie. She jumps and grabs the hands of two men sitting beside her.

Driven/r

Desperation drove us to it. It being
        to do what eyes do. Which is register
the edge of our furthest limits, out
        the yellow line coming at you, though
beyond the median. It matters little
        we know that's not true. For the road
in retrospect, but in the moment
        is static, and what moves is you in
it mattered greatly, because people die
        the car, you who have your hand on
in such circumstances they surrender.
        the wheel, your foot on the pedal
That is to say we were desperate driving
        or beside it if you've engaged cruise
that two-lane highway for days on end-
        control. You see the hand and know it
of-days until the yellow line imprinted
        is yours despite feeling no connection
itself in our minds or our eyes or
        to it or anything approaching feeling.
both. Who could tell the difference?
        Just as you know your feet are present
Who would want to? Minds don't see
        whether you see or feel them. Feet are
per se. They only reflect on experience
        habitual. Hands, also. But you're
arrived at by way of the senses. When dead
        as good as dead that moment.
tired, when your body has conformed
        Disembodied some might say. Only
itself to the seats in whatever automobile

you happen to be driving, when it
we don't say such things, this we not
reaches that particular equilibrium
driving but driven by us. Not even
where   you   feel   every   ligament
when the yellow line flickers and flits,
strain, even your eyes in your head
leaving us without medium, adrift,
(wherever your mind resides) struggle
traveling   at   indeterminate   speeds.

The Hour of Lead

If more luminous the stars
                around the moon
she might gaze upward
                      and voices like damp fingers

might blister her retina remembering
                coalesce into swirls that eddy
the names of constellations
                      press her forehead with glue

and the heroic tales imposed on them
                streetlights their heads
this wearied woman
                      that binds memory dimmed

possessed-possessing her form
                like cockscomb mutant
who waltzes through this city's
                      faintest flickers until rain

mottled incandescence
                faces atop erect necks
might forget herself a moment
                      begins and she extends a hand

what he did to her what she said
                lips parted the stars nearly
to him might hum the words
                      for what will puddle in creases

she didn't say gazing past
                transparent without consequence
this platform of timbers and metal
                      of her palm lines stretched

tracks that cast shadows
                    viewed through mute yellow glow
on the cars and figures below
                              to tributaries paisley welts

much as the train's rhythmic grind
                    she holds a frayed hem
overwhelms the riotous birds
                              where grease spattered

indignant lullabies or mists
                    of sleeve against her cheek

                              her forearms

After Years Of Misuse We Abandon Language
For Unornamented Flower Pots

The flowers are incidental: meaning conveyed
by shape and size, the hue of fired clay, crackle of glaze.

Each pot distinct, a lingua formed frankly
by the potter's fingers, each singular in breadth and reach.

Everyday niceties require a skid loader.

Broken ones are mourned, their shards placed in boxes
and buried in individual graves.

Certain vessels become legendary for what they can say.
They are auctioned, traded and stolen. Passable forgeries
become priceless.

These are not the pots you would imagine. They express
the most mundane desires...

I wish to know you.

Please, leave.

My hands ache from cold.

§

Postlogue

Poetry... It's what heals you.

Side Effects of This Poem May Include: *abdominal pain, abnormal dreams or thoughts, acne, aggression, agitation, allergic reaction, altered taste, anxiety, back pain, balance issues, blindness, blurred vision, brain zaps, breast development in males, breast pain or enlargement, breathing difficulties, bruise-like marks on the skin, cataracts, changeable emotions, chest pain, clammy skin, cold, concentration impairment, conjunctivitis (i.e., pinkeye), constipation, coughing, crying spells, decreased appetite, decreased sex drive, depersonalization, diarrhea or loose stools, difficulty breathing, difficulty swallowing, difficulty with ejaculation, dizziness, electric shock sensations, double vision, dry eyes, dry mouth, exaggerated feeling of well-being, eye pain, fainting, fatigue, feeling faint upon arising from a sitting or lying position, female and male sexual problems, fever, flatulence, fluid retention, flu-like symptoms, flushing, frequent urination, gas, hair loss, hallucinations, headache, hearing problems, heart attack, hemorrhage or discharge, hemorrhoids, hiccups, high blood pressure, high pressure within the eye (glaucoma), hostility, hot flushes, impaired concentration, impaired speech, impotence, inability to stay seated, increased appetite, increased salivation, increased sex drive, increased sweating, indigestion, inflamed nasal passages, inflammation of the penis, insomnia, intolerance to light, irregular heartbeat, irritability, itching, joint pains, jumpy nerves, kidney failure, lack of coordination, lack of sensation, leg cramps, lethargy, low blood pressure, memory loss, menstrual problems, migraine headaches, movement problems, muscle cramps or weakness, nausea, need to urinate during the night, nervousness, nosebleed, out-of-control behavior called mania or the similar but less dramatic hyper" state called hypomania, over-reacting to situations, pain upon urination, paranoia, prolonged erection, purplish spots on the skin, racing heartbeat, rapid mood shifts, rash, rectal hemorrhage, repetitive thoughts or songs, respiratory infection/lung problems, ringing in the ears, rolling eyes, sensitivity to light, sensory & sleep disturbances, severe internal restlessness (i.e., akathasia), sinus inflammation, skin eruptions, sleepiness, sleepwalking, sore throat, sores on tongue, speech problems, stomach and intestinal inflammation, stomach cramps, suicidal thoughts, swelling of the face and throat, swollen wrists and ankles, thirst, throbbing heartbeat, tingling or pins and needles, tinnitus (i.e., ear ringing or buzzing), tooth-grinding, tremors, troubling thoughts, twitching, "unreal" feeling, vaginal inflammation, vision problems, visual hallucinations/illusions, vivid dreams, vomiting, worsened depression, and yawning.*

End

Notes

"Prologue: At The Observation Pavilion" is constructed from patient reports as quoted in August Hoch's *Benign Stupors* (1921).

"Victory and Opposites," "Shut Down Up," "Field Stone," "Modern Life," "Natural Light," "Fate of Humanity," and "Character" were all constructed using a found text operation. For each, a favorite book title was entered into the Amazon.com search engine, and the poem was then constructed using only text found in the three-line excerpts provided for the various search results. After compiling the available text, the process was something not unlike "automatic writing." With gratitude to Amy England, Mark Nowak, Catherine Kasper, Matthea Harvey, Michael Anania, Frank Rogaczewski and Jena Osman.

"A Problem of Localization: Leaving vs. Relocating" references by way of its title Baron Constantin von Economovon San Serff's 1929 Lecture "Sleep as a Problem of Localization."

"The Somnambulist Awakens To Discover" was inspired by Alex Williams's article "The Mysteries of Tobias Wong" (New York Times, June 25, 2010).

"Pi: A Drama with Theatrical Limits" is inspired by Daniel Tamment's descriptions of his "ordinal linguistic personification," a form of synethesia where positive integers (up to 10,000 for Tamment) each have particular colors, shapes and textures, essentially their own personality or character. Tamment holds the European Record for reciting Pi, which he did to 22,514 places as part of a fund-raiser for the National Society for Epilepsy. Tamment is the author of: *Born on a Blue Day: Inside the Extraordinary Mind of an Autistic Savant* (2007) and *Embracing the Wide Sky: A Tour Across the Horizons of the Mind* (2009).

"Night Terrors: Men Watch (and Women)" and "Night Terrors: Dahlia Jarezii" both appropriate text from the IMDB "Parent's Guide"—the first for the movie *Watchmen* (2009), and the second for the movie *Black Dahlia* (2009). The author has never seen either of these films.

"This Poem Will Put Hair on Your Chi-Chi" compiles major and minor side-effects for the drug Rogaine. "Postlogue" compiles major and minor side-effects of the antidepressant drug Zoloft.

"Some Nights I Expire" owes a debt of gratitude to Jericho Brown.

Acknowledgments

The author wishes to thank the editors of *Eleven Eleven, The 2011 Houston Poetry Fest Anthology, Pebble Lake Review,* and *Fifth Wednesday Journal* who published poems in this manuscript (or versions thereof), and also Vincent Toro for including two poems in the Guadalupe Cultural Arts Center's "Verses" installation at the Torpicana Hotel.

Special thanks, as well, to Hsin-I Liu and Elaine Wong [a.ka.the Late Huang Favorite Team] for their nine cows and two tigers worth of translation efforts. Thanks also to Amy England and Wendy Barker for their editorial feedback, and to Dana Curtis and Duriel Harris for giving this book life. And as always, the author wishes to thank Catherine Kasper, his partner in everything.

TITLES FROM ELIXIR PRESS